Your Guide to Spices and Seasonings

Discover How to Make Your Own Spices and Seasonings at Home!

BY: Valeria Ray

License Notes

Copyright © 2020 Valeria Ray All Rights Reserved

All rights to the content of this book are reserved by the Author without exception unless permission is given stating otherwise.

The Author have no claims as to the authenticity of the content and the Reader bears all responsibility and risk when following the content. The Author is not liable for any reparations, damages, accidents, injuries or other incidents occurring from the Reader following all or part of this publication.

Table of Contents

Introduction 6

    Lahori Seasoning 7

    Spicy Curry Seasoning 9

    Lamb Seasoning 11

    Berbere 13

    Chinese Five-Spice Powder 15

    Khmeli-Suneli 17

    Curry Powder 19

    Chili Powder 21

    Za'atar 23

    Kansas City Dry Rub 25

    Gomasio 27

    Togarashi 29

    Herbes De Provence 31

    Cajun Seasoning Blend 33

Jerk Seasoning Blend 35

Mediterranean Seasoning Blend 37

Salt-Free All-Purpose Seasoning Blend 39

Ranch Seasoning Blend 41

Homemade Poultry Seasoning Mix 43

Italian Seasoning Blend 45

Taco and Fajita Seasoning Blend\ 47

Pumpkin Spice Mix 49

Everything Bagel Seasoning 51

Sazón 53

Montreal Steak Spice Mix 55

Crudités with Chile Lime Salt 57

Ras-El-Hanout 59

Lebkuchen Spice Mix 61

Sriracha Salt 63

Tandoori Spice Blend 65

Conclusion 67

About the Author 68

Author's Afterthoughts 69

Introduction

Whether you're looking to spice up your old recipes or want to learn how to make your own spices at home, this book is a must-have in your kitchen. With the help of this book, you'll be able to concoct amazing spice and seasoning recipes that will take any dish you make to the next level!

What's more, all the recipes in this book are super easy to make and can be made by anyone! They all come with simple instructions and can easily be doubled or tripled.

So, what are you waiting for? Let's begin!

Lahori Seasoning

Enjoy the flavors of Pakistan in any meal with this seasoning recipe!

Makes: ½ cup

Prep: 5 mins

Ingredients:

- 2 tbsp. cumin seeds
- 5 tbsp. cilantro seeds
- 5 tbsp. chickpea flour
- 1 tbsp. chili flakes
- 1 tbsp. fenugreek
- 1 tbsp. turmeric

Directions:

Mix all the spices in a bowl. Use as needed.

Spicy Curry Seasoning

This spicy seasoning is sure to bring a kick to anything you add it to!

Makes: 3 tbsp.

Prep: 5 mins

Ingredients:

- ¼ teaspoon ground turmeric
- ⅛ teaspoon cayenne
- ½ teaspoon ground coriander
- ½ teaspoon paprika
- ¼ teaspoon curry powder
- 2 teaspoons fresh thyme leaves, lightly chopped
- ⅛ teaspoon salt

Directions:

Mix all the spices in a bowl. Use as needed.

Lamb Seasoning

This seasoning recipe is perfect for lamb or any other red meat!

Makes: ¼ cup

Prep: 5 mins

Ingredients:

- ½ teaspoon paprika
- ½ teaspoon ground cumin
- ¼ teaspoon ground turmeric
- 2 cloves garlic, minced
- 1 teaspoon ground coriander
- Salt and freshly ground black pepper
- 2 tablespoons finely chopped
- Parsley (about 5 sprigs)

Directions:

Mix all the spices in a bowl. Use as needed.

Berbere

Berbere is a bright-orange spice mix of Ethiopian origin. The Berbere spice mix can be used for a wide variety of foods, from chicken and pork to pies and French fries.

Makes: 1 cup

Prep: 15 mins

Ingredients:

- ½ cup dried, powdered New Mexico Chili
- ¼ cup paprika
- 1 tbsp. Cayenne Pepper
- 1 tsp Onion powder
- 1 tsp ground ginger
- 1 tsp cumin
- 1 tsp powdered coriander
- ½ tsp powdered garlic
- 1 tsp powdered fenugreek
- 1 tsp powdered cardamom
- ½ tsp powdered allspice
- ½ tsp powdered cloves
- ¼ tsp powdered nutmeg
- ½ tsp milled cinnamon

Directions:

First, add the powdered chili, cayenne pepper and paprika into a bowl, and stir thoroughly.

Then, add in your onion powder, ginger, allspice, cloves, nutmeg cinnamon, powdered garlic, fenugreek, cardamom, coriander and cumin to the prepared mixture in the bowl.

Carefully but firmly, whip all the ingredients in the bowl together until all the ingredients are fully blended. Fine bright-orange powder with a fine consistency should be achieved.

The final Berbere mix may then be stored in a firmly closed airtight container and used for a wide variety of meals.

Chinese Five-Spice Powder

This five-spice powder can easily be incorporated into noodles, chicken wings, grilled BBQ, and even rice.

Makes: 1/3 cup

Prep: 10 minutes

Ingredients:

- 1 tsp powdered cinnamon
- 1 tsp crushed anise seeds
- ¼ tsp crushed fennel seeds
- ¼ tsp powdered fresh pepper
- 1/8 tsp powdered cloves

Directions:

Gather your ground cinnamon, anise seeds, fennel seeds, fresh pepper and cloves in a bowl.

Mix thoroughly until a fine, homogenous blend is achieved.

Keep your spice mix in an airtight container. The result of this recipe gives 3 teaspoons of the Chinese five-spice powder.

Khmeli-Suneli

This fantastic spice mix from Georgia is a true treasure to behold.

Makes: 14 tbsp.

Prep: 5 min

Ingredients:

- 2 tbsp. dried summer savory
- 1 tbsp. dried fenugreek leaves
- 2 tbsp. crushed coriander
- 2 tbsp. dried mint
- 2 tbsp. dry marjoram
- 2 tsp dried and crushed marigold petals
- 2 tbsp. dried dill
- 1 tsp ground black pepper
- 2 tbsp. dried parsley
- 1 tsp crushed fenugreek seeds
- 2 pcs ground bay leaves

Directions:

Simply combine all ingredients in the right proportions in a ceramic or glass bowl.

Mix all the ingredients together, firmly but gently until a fine, even consistency is achieved.

Store your spice mix in an airtight container. This recipe makes 1 cup of Khmeli-Suneli.

Curry Powder

Learn to make curry powder with the help of this easy recipe!

Makes: 1/3 cup

Prep: 5 mins

Ingredients:

- 2 tbsp. powdered coriander
- 2 tbsp. powdered cumin
- 1½ tbsp. powdered turmeric
- 2 tsp powdered ginger
- 1 tsp dried mustard
- ½ tsp crushed black pepper
- 1 tsp powdered cinnamon
- ½ tsp crushed cardamom
- ½ tsp ground cayenne pepper

Directions:

Assemble all collected spices into a small bowl.

Stir thoroughly until an even consistency is achieved.

Pour the curry powder into a small glass or ceramic jar.

Shake thoroughly to ensure homogeneity.

Store in the airtight jar. Curry powder can be preserved, if kept away from air and moisture, for up to three months.

Chili Powder

Chili powder has been traditionally used to make popular chili dishes for hundreds of years and for good reasons!

Makes: 1/3 cup

Prep: 5 mins

Ingredients:

- 1/8 cup Sweet paprika
- ½ tsp smoked paprika (optional)
- 1½ tsp grounded garlic
- ½ tsp grounded cayenne pepper
- 1½ grounded onion spice
- 1 tsp dried oregano
- 1 tsp milled cumin

Directions:

Add all ingredients into ceramic or glass bowl.

Mix gently but thoroughly until an even, fine consistency is achieved.

Store the mixture in an airtight container. This incredible homemade spice may be stored for up to a year if kept away from air and moisture.

Za'atar

The Za'atar spice mix is a fantastic blend of exotic and local spices that can be used for a ton of cooking applications. This spice, which is of Middle Eastern origin, may be used as a rub for chicken, fish, and beef, and combines perfectly with olive oil to produce an exotic-tasting marinade.

Makes: ½ cup

Prep: 5 mins

Ingredients:

- 1 tbsp. crushed thyme
- 1 tbsp. Powdered cumin
- 1 tbsp. Powdered coriander
- 1 tbsp. Heated and ground sesame seeds
- 1 tbsp. Sumac
- ½ tsp kosher salt
- ¼ tsp Aleppo chili flakes (optional)

Directions:

Heat whole sesame, coriander and cumin seeds if the whole seeds are available. If they are not, then powdered spices may be used instead.

Assemble listed ingredients in a small glass or ceramic bowl.

Mix the spices thoroughly until a fine, even consistency is achieved.

Store in an airtight jar.

Kansas City Dry Rub

This spice mix from the sunny city of Kansas has been in use for decades as an ever-reliable and unique rub for Barbecued pork ribs. The dry rub can, however, also be used to spice up your chicken and beef.

Makes: 12 servings

Prep: 40 mins

Ingredients:

- ¼ cup paprika
- ½ cup brown sugar
- 1 tbsp. black pepper
- 1 tbsp. powdered cayenne pepper
- 1 tbsp. ground garlic
- 1 tbsp. chili powder
- 1 tbsp. ground onions
- 1 tbsp. table salt

Directions:

Assemble all in a small glass/ceramic bowl.

Mix all constituent spices thoroughly until a homogenous mixture is gotten

Store the resultant mixture in an airtight jar away from moisture.

Gomasio

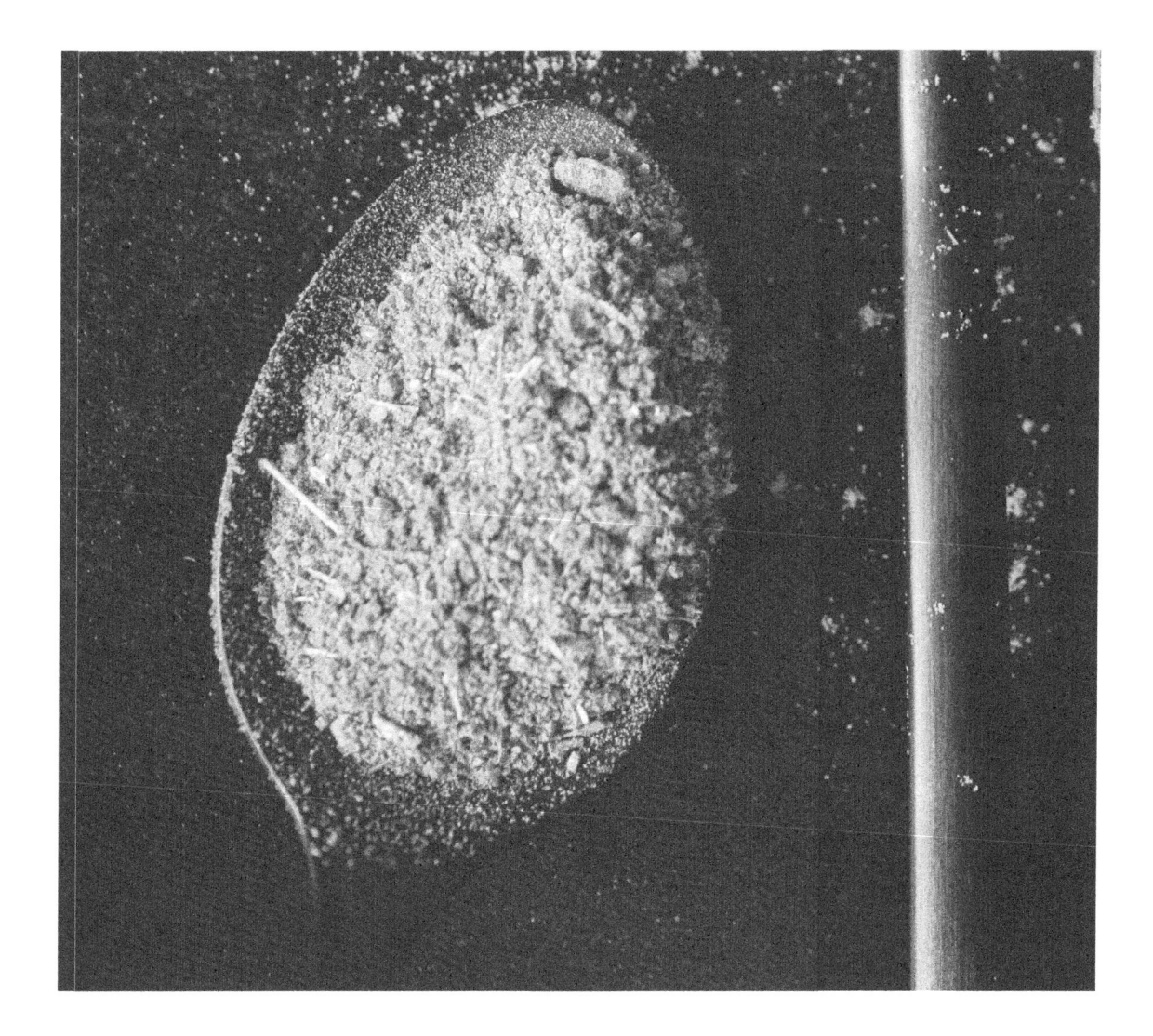

Gomasio is a Japanese spice mix reputable for its distinctive taste and its healing properties. It is probably one of the easiest spice mixes of all time to make.

Makes: 32 servings

Prep: 20 mins

Ingredients:

- 1 tbsp. Celtic sea salt
- 2 cups whole sesame seeds

Directions:

Using a cast-iron skillet to roast your whole sesame seeds over medium heat for 10 minutes.

Pour your roast sesame seeds into a mortar and add the Celtic salt.

Pound the mixture of the sesame seeds and the salt in the mortar until an even, fine consistency is achieved.

Pour the spice mix into an airtight glass jar, and store for up to 3 weeks, preferably in a refrigerator.

Togarashi

Togarashi is made from seven unique constituent spices and confers a deliciously enticing flavor to foods from different kinds – from noodles and grilled chicken to stews and soups. Whatever dish you are trying to create, the Togarashi spice blend promises to make it extraordinary.

Makes: 1 cup

Prep: 10 mins

Ingredients:

- 2 tbsp. red Chili Powder
- 1 tbsp. dried and crushed orange peels
- 2 tsp ground white sesame seeds
- 2 tsp ground black sesame seeds
- 1 tsp Sichuan or Sancho peppercorns
- 1 tsp grounded ginger
- ½ tsp crushed poppy seeds
- ½ sheet crumbled toasted nori

Directions:

Assemble the white and black sesame seeds, the Sichuan or Sancho peppercorns, and the whole poppy seeds in a dry skillet, and heat gently until they become fragrant.

Transfer the heated ingredients to a grinder and pulse them gently until a coarse consistency is achieved.

Store your coarse spice mix in a sealed glass or ceramic jar away from air or moisture. For best results, the Togarashi spice should be used within three weeks of preparation.

Herbes De Provence

Herbes de Provence is one of the finest and most remarkable spice blends in the world.

Makes: 11 tbsp.

Prep: 5 mins

Ingredients:

- 2 tbsp. dried savory
- 3 tbsp. dried thyme
- 2 tbsp. powdered oregano
- 2 tbsp. dried parsley
- 1 tbsp. dried rosemary
- 1 tbsp. dried marjoram
- 1 tbsp. dried lavender flowers

Directions:

All constituent spices are to be assembled in a bowl and mixed gently but thoroughly.

To achieve a finer consistency, the mix of herbs may be grounded using a grinder or a mortar and pestle.

The spice blend may then be stored in an airtight container.

Cajun Seasoning Blend

The homemade version of the infamous Cajun spice mix gives a stronger and more distinctive flavor than the ones on the shelves, and the absence of preservatives and filters makes it a lot healthier.

Makes: ½ cup

Prep: 10 min

Ingredients:

- 2½ tbsp. sea salt
- 1 tbsp. oregano
- 1 tbsp. paprika
- 1 tbsp. cayenne pepper
- 1 tbsp. black pepper
- 1 tsp onion powder
- 1 tsp garlic powder

Directions:

Assemble all listed ingredients into a glass or ceramic bowl.

Stir all the ingredients together thoroughly until an even, fine consistency is achieved.

Use as needed.

Jerk Seasoning Blend

The jerk seasoning blend has a touch of exotic splendor to every single meal and can be used for a variety of soups, stews, and meats.

Makes: ½ cup

Prep: 10 mins

Ingredients:

- 3 tbsp. dried minced onions
- 1 tbsp. thyme
- 1 tbsp. allspice
- 1 tbsp. black pepper
- 1 tsp cinnamon
- 1 tsp cayenne pepper
- ½ tsp sea salt
- 1 tsp garlic powder

Directions:

Assemble all listed ingredients into a glass or ceramic bowl.

Whisk all the ingredients together thoroughly until an even, fine consistency is achieved.

Use as needed.

Mediterranean Seasoning Blend

The Mediterranean seasoning blend goes well with meat, poultry, fish, and vegetable-based dishes.

Makes: ½ cup

Prep: 10 mins

Ingredients:

- 2 tbsp. basil
- 2 tbsp. oregano
- 2 tbsp. kosher salt
- 1 tbsp. parsley flakes
- 1 tbsp. dried onions
- 1 tsp black pepper

Directions:

Pour your basil, kosher salt, dried oregano, parsley flakes, dried onions and black pepper into a glass or ceramic bowl.

Using a whisk, mix all spices thoroughly until a fine, homogenous mixture is attained.

Carefully transfer the spices into an airtight jar, and store in a cool, dry place.

Salt-Free All-Purpose Seasoning Blend

This seasoning blend is most remarkable for its healthiness.

Makes: ½ cup

Prep: 10 mins

Ingredients:

- 2 tbsp. grounded garlic
- 2 tbsp. onion powder
- 1 tbsp. grounded chili
- 1 tbsp. paprika
- 1 tbsp. parsley
- 1½ tsp black pepper

Directions:

Pour all ingredients into a glass/ceramic bowl.

Mix the ingredients with a ladle until you get an even consistency.

Transfer into an airtight jar and store.

Ranch Seasoning Blend

This homemade blend is a brilliant, healthier, and way more affordable alternative to the expensive ranch seasoning mix packets sold at grocery stores.

Makes: 1 cup

Prep: 10 mins

Ingredients:

- 5 tbsp. parsley
- 4 tsp grounded dill
- 5 tsp grounded garlic
- 5 tsp onion powder
- 6 tsp dried onions
- 2 tsp black pepper
- 3 tsp sea salt

Directions:

Find a glass or ceramic bowl and dump the ingredients into it.

Stir consistently until you have a fine mixture.

Pour the spice blend into a jar and store. Keep covered.

Homemade Poultry Seasoning Mix

This superb homemade poultry spice mix is affordable, easy to make, and perfect for the preparation of all types of poultry – turkey, chicken, duck, and even pheasants.

Makes: 6 tbsp.

Prep: 5 mins

Ingredients:

- 2 tbsp. powdered sage
- 1½ tbsp. thyme
- 1 tbsp. Marjoram
- 1 tbsp. rosemary
- ½ tbsp. nutmeg
- ½ tbsp. black pepper

Directions:

Gather your ingredients and pour them inside a glass or ceramic bowl.

Mix together gently until you have a fine mixture.

Find an airtight jar and transfer the mixture into it.

Italian Seasoning Blend

The Italian spice mix can be used for a variety of foods – soups, stews, and meats. The Italian seasoning blend is also very easy to make and is highly affordable.

Makes: ½ cup

Prep: 10 mins

Ingredients:

- 4 tsp. basil
- 4 tsp. oregano
- 4 tsp. rosemary
- 4 tsp. marjoram
- 4 tsp. thyme
- 4 tsp. savory
- 2 tsp. grounded garlic

Directions:

The first thing to do is to get your ingredients ready. Now, get a glass or ceramic bowl and pour the ingredients inside.

Stir together to achieve an even consistency.

You are done. Get them into an airtight container or jar and store.

Taco and Fajita Seasoning Blend\

This spice mix is perfect for tacos, casseroles, chili, and even meats, and it has a low sodium content making it perfect for individuals conscious about their salt intakes.

Makes: ½ cup

Prep: 10 mins

Ingredients:

- 2 tsp. grounded chili
- 2 tsp. coriander
- 4 tsp. cumin
- 1 tsp. grounded onions
- 1 tsp. grounded garlic
- 1 tsp. oregano
- 2 tsp. sea salt
- 1 tsp. smoked paprika
- ½ tsp. grounded black pepper
- ¼ tsp. grounded chipotle chili

Directions:

Collect all the ingredients and pour them into a bowl.

Mix together thoroughly until you get a fine blend.

Transfer the mix into a container and keep tightly covered. Store in a cool and dry place.

Pumpkin Spice Mix

Make your own pumpkin spice mix with the help of this recipe!

Makes: 6 tbsp.

Prep: 5 mins

Ingredients:

- 3 tbsp. cinnamon
- 2 tbsp. powdered ginger
- 1 tsp. ground allspice
- 1 tsp. powdered nutmeg
- ½ tsp. powdered cloves

Directions:

Assemble all listed ingredients into a glass or ceramic bowl.

Whisk all the ingredients together thoroughly until an even, fine consistency is achieved.

Use as needed.

Everything Bagel Seasoning

This incredible spice blend incorporates a variety of native and exotic spices and crushed seeds to give a simply stunning taste to a wide variety of dishes it can be used for.

Makes: ¾ cup

Prep: 5 mins

Ingredients:

- 3 tbsp. poppy seeds
- 3 tbsp. sesame seeds
- 2 tbsp. dried and chopped garlic
- 2 tbsp. chopped and dried onions
- 3 tbsp. rough salt

Directions:

Heat up your sesame seeds, poppy seeds, dried garlic and onions over medium heat in a small skillet. Stir the heating mixture continuously until a distinctive smell and a light brown coloration of the spice blend is observed.

Pour the spice blend into a glass or ceramic bowl, add in the salt, and stir the resultant thoroughly.

Let cool and then move to an airtight jar. The spice blend must be kept in a cool, dry place, and should preferably be stored at room temp for not more than a month.

Sazón

Sazón can be used to prepare soups, stews, braises, and the seasoning of different meat products – chicken, ham, lamb, and even fish.

Makes: ½ cup

Prep: 3 mins

Ingredients:

- 1 tbsp. powdered garlic
- 1 tbsp. onion powder
- 1 tbsp. grounded cumin
- 1 tbsp. powdered turmeric
- ½ tbsp. ground black pepper
- 2 tbsp. salt
- 2 tbsp. sweet paprika

Directions:

Add all listed ingredients into a bowl and whisk thoroughly until an even, homogenous mixture is attained.

Transfer the spice blend into an airtight bowl, and store in a cool, dark and dry place.

Montreal Steak Spice Mix

This vintage spice blend is a true classic, and it promises to add a taste of antique excitement to every meal you use it for.

Makes: ½ cup

Prep: 10 mins

Ingredients:

- 2 tbsp. black peppercorns
- 1 tbsp. mustard seeds
- 2 tsp. dill seeds
- 1 tsp. coriander seeds
- 1 tbsp. + 1 tsp kosher salt
- 1 tbsp. + 1 tsp dried and chopped garlic
- 1 tsp. crushed red pepper flakes

Directions:

In a small skillet, heat the peppercorns, mustard seeds, dill seeds, and coriander seeds at medium heat.

Stir the mixture in the skillet continuously until a distinctive aroma is detected. The seeds should begin to pop after 2 minutes.

Pour the gritty mixture into a mortar and crush further with a pestle.

Add in your salt, garlic, and chili grits, and crush all ingredients until your desired consistency is achieved.

Transfer the mixture into an airtight jar, keep in a cool, dry place, and use within a month of preparation.

Crudités with Chile Lime Salt

This exotic spice blend helps to add a touch of tangy zest to every single dish. This mix is, however, mostly used as a dip for raw fruits and vegetables.

Makes: 10 servings

Prep: 30 mins

Ingredients:

- 1 lime
- 2 tbsp. coarse sea salt
- ½ tsp. ancho chile powder
- 2 oranges
- 5 small, seedless cucumbers
- 1 bunch of radishes
- Large jicama

Directions:

Cut up your oranges into small 1/4 inch rounds and cut up each round in half.

Cut your cucumber into ½ inch bits

Cut up all radishes in halves.

Peel the jicama, cut it into ¼-inch thick slices. Then further cut half the slices into semi-circles, and the other slices into triangles.

Peel your lime and process the lime zest into a small bowl. Add in your salt and chili powder into the bowl and stir thoroughly.

Cut the lime into wedges and arrange all other ingredients on a platter. Squeeze the lime juice onto the assortment of ingredients and sprinkle in the spiced salt mixture.

Serve the spice mix alongside the remaining spice salt.

Ras-El-Hanout

This vibrant and versatile spice mix has its origin in the dry plains of Morocco in North Africa. It is commonly used in the preparation of roast chicken or grilled lamb.

Makes: 2 tbsp.

Prep: 5 mins

Ingredients:

- 1 tsp. cumin
- 1 tsp. ground ginger
- ¾ tsp. ground black pepper
- ¼ tsp. ground cloves
- ½ tsp. ground coriander
- 1 tsp. salt
- ½ tsp. powdered cayenne pepper
- ½ tsp. powdered cinnamon
- ½ tsp. ground allspice

Directions:

Get your ceramic bowl or anything similar and pour the ingredients into the base.

Mix gently but consistently until you get a fine blend.

Now, transfer the content to an airtight container. Always keep covered.

Lebkuchen Spice Mix

Lebkuchen spice mix is widely used to give cinnamon rolls, and glazed apple cakes their uniquely irresistible tastes. Each ingredient that makes up this spice blend can be altered in quantity to give just the right, desired flavor.

Makes: ½ cup

Prep: 5 mins

Ingredients:

- 5 tbsp. ground cinnamon
- 1 tsp. ground allspice
- 1 tsp. ground mace
- ¾ tsp. crushed aniseed
- 1½ tbsp. ground cloves

Directions:

Gather all the ingredients and dump them into a bowl.

Mix with a ladle or anything utensil until you get a fine consistency.

Remove the mixture from the bowl and transfer to an airtight container. Keep away from moisture and direct sunlight.

This resilient spice can retain its distinct flavor for up to one year.

Sriracha Salt

The Sriracha salt blend can be used to spice up just about anything – popcorn, noodles, fried potatoes, and even fruits and veggies.

Makes: 1 cup

Prep: 24 hrs.

Ingredients:

- 2 tbsp. sriracha sauce
- 1 cup unrefined sea salt

Directions:

Stir the salt and the sauce thoroughly until an even mixture is achieved.

Spread the mixture on a dry baking sheet, and place in an oven set to 100°F overnight.

Remove the dried mixture from the oven and crush the lumps with a spoon until a fine consistency is attained.

Store the blend in an airtight jar and keep away from moisture.

Tandoori Spice Blend

This brightly colored spice mix packs a unique tangy taste, a stunning flavor, and can be used for a wide range of foods. It is, however, popularly used as a rub for different meat types – chicken, beef, ham, and sometimes, fish.

Makes: Approx. 2 tbsp.

Prep: 5 mins

Ingredients:

- 1 tsp. ground ginger
- 1 tsp. ground cayenne pepper
- 1 tsp. ground cumin
- 1 tsp. powdered coriander
- 1 tsp. ground turmeric
- 1 tsp. paprika
- 1 tsp. table salt

Directions:

Find a bowl, put all the ingredients into it, and mix gently but consistently until you get a fine blend.

Transfer the even mixture into an airtight jar and use within two weeks of preparation.

Conclusion

Well, there you go! Amazing spice and seasoning recipes for you to liven up your daily dishes! Make sure to try out all the seasonings in this book because you never know which one will turn out to be your favorite!

About the Author

A native of Indianapolis, Indiana, Valeria Ray found her passion for cooking while she was studying English Literature at Oakland City University. She decided to try a cooking course with her friends and the experience changed her forever. She enrolled at the Art Institute of Indiana which offered extensive courses in the culinary Arts. Once Ray dipped her toe in the cooking world, she never looked back.

When Valeria graduated, she worked in French restaurants in the Indianapolis area until she became the head chef at one of the 5-star establishments in the area. Valeria's attention to taste and visual detail caught the eye of a local business person who expressed an interest in publishing her recipes. Valeria began her secondary career authoring cookbooks and e-books which she tackled with as much talent and gusto as her first career. Her passion for food leaps off the page of her books which have colourful anecdotes and stunning pictures of dishes she has prepared herself.

Valeria Ray lives in Indianapolis with her husband of 15 years, Tom, her daughter, Isobel and their loveable Golden Retriever, Goldy. Valeria enjoys cooking special dishes in her large, comfortable kitchen where the family gets involved in preparing meals. This successful, dynamic chef is an inspiration to culinary students and novice cooks everywhere.

Author's Afterthoughts

Thank you for Purchasing my book and taking the time to read it from front to back. I am always grateful when a reader chooses my work and I hope you enjoyed it!

With the vast selection available online, I am touched that you chose to be purchasing my work and take valuable time out of your life to read it. My hope is that you feel you made the right decision.

I very much would like to know what you thought of the book. Please take the time to write an honest and informative review on Amazon.com. Your experience and opinions will be of great benefit to me and those readers looking to make an informed choice.

With much thanks,

Valeria Ray

Made in the USA
Middletown, DE
10 March 2025